MW00896528

TREES!

A MY INCREDIBLE WORLD PICTURE BOOK

MY INCREDIBLE WORLD

Copyright © 2024, My Incredible World

All rights reserved. This book or any portion thereof may not be reproduced or used in any manner whatsoever without the express written permission of the copyright holder.

www.myincredibleworld.com

Trees are tall, woody plants
with branches, leaves, and roots
that are vital to life on Earth.

Trees are the longest-living
organisms on Earth, with some
living thousands of years!

The oldest known tree, a bristle-cone pine in a secret location in California, is over 4,800 years old!

Trees absorb carbon dioxide from the air and release oxygen, helping us breathe.

A single mature tree can provide
enough oxygen for up to
four people in one day!

Trees can communicate with each other through their roots using a network of fungi.

This "Wood Wide Web" helps trees share nutrients and send warnings about pests.

There are over 60,000 species of trees around the world.

The Amazon Rainforest alone is home to about 16,000 different species of trees!

Trees help prevent soil erosion by holding the soil in place with their roots.

Their leaves help filter the
air by trapping dust and
absorbing pollutants.

The tallest tree in the world is a coast redwood named Hyperion, standing 380 feet tall.

The largest tree by volume is the General Sherman, a giant sequoia weighing 2.7 million pounds!

Trees can cool the environment by providing shade and releasing water vapor through their leaves.

A single tree can reduce the temperature in its surrounding area by up to 10°F (5.6°C).

Deciduous trees lose their leaves
in autumn to conserve water
during the winter.

Evergreen trees keep their leaves
or needles all year round,
even in freezing temperatures.

Trees can live in almost every environment, from deserts to rainforests and mountain tops.

They are an essential habitat for countless animals, from birds to insects to mammals.

Trees have growth rings that tell us their age and the conditions they've lived through.

Scientists use tree rings to study past weather and climate!

Trees are incredible!

Made in the USA
Las Vegas, NV
03 December 2024

13236420R00017